CHOW MANE

WRITTEN BY ANDRÉA ZIMMERMAN
ILLUSTRATED BY ALAIN DAIGLE

Library and Archives Canada Cataloguing in Publications.

Illustrations by Alain Daigle.

For permission contact
info@a-zdigital.com
Print ISBN: 978-1-7776323-0-4
1st Edition

I DEDICATE THIS TO
KAYLIEGH QUINN HAMBLIN
(PANDA)
IN LOVING MEMORY OF HER FATHER.

MONEY MADE FROM THIS POETRY
WILL CONTINUE GOOD DEEDS
DONATIONS WILL BE PAID
TO MORE ANIMALS IN NEED.

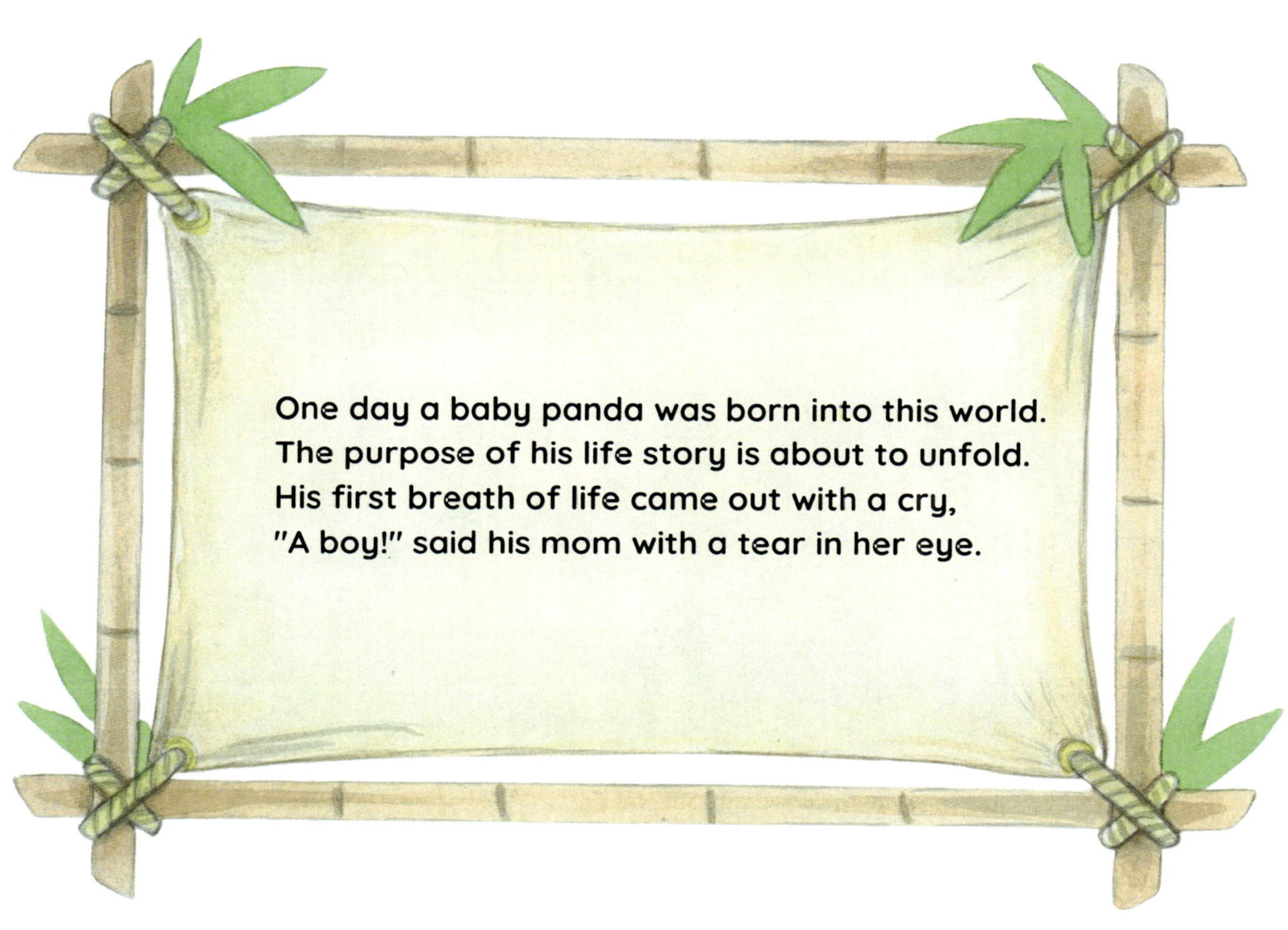

One day a baby panda was born into this world.
The purpose of his life story is about to unfold.
His first breath of life came out with a cry,
"A boy!" said his mom with a tear in her eye.

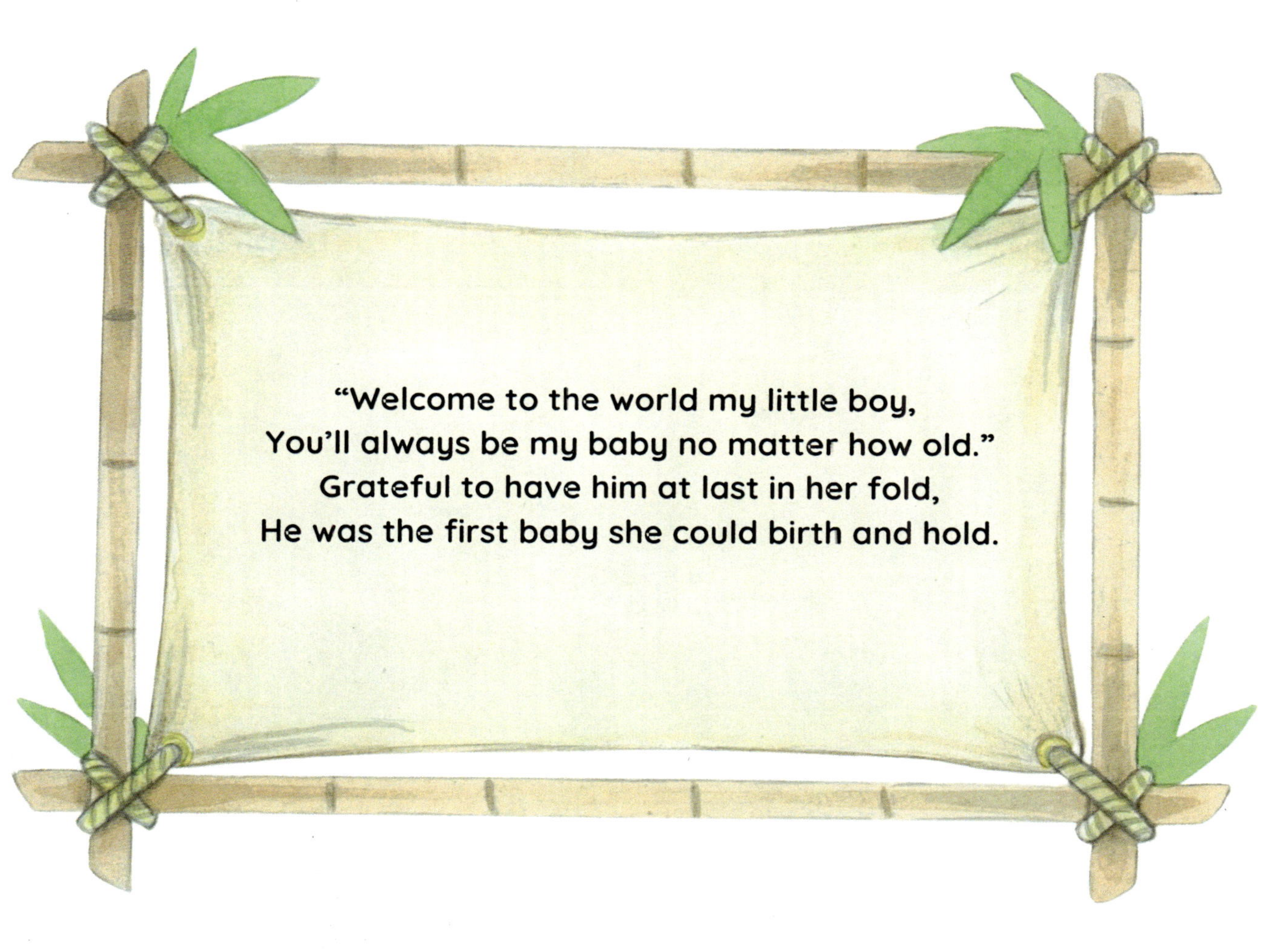

“Welcome to the world my little boy,
You’ll always be my baby no matter how old.”
Grateful to have him at last in her fold,
He was the first baby she could birth and hold.

"Here in China's forested land,
I will raise you from cub as best as I can."

Together they roamed their bamboo jungle,
Climbing trees and having downhill tumbles.

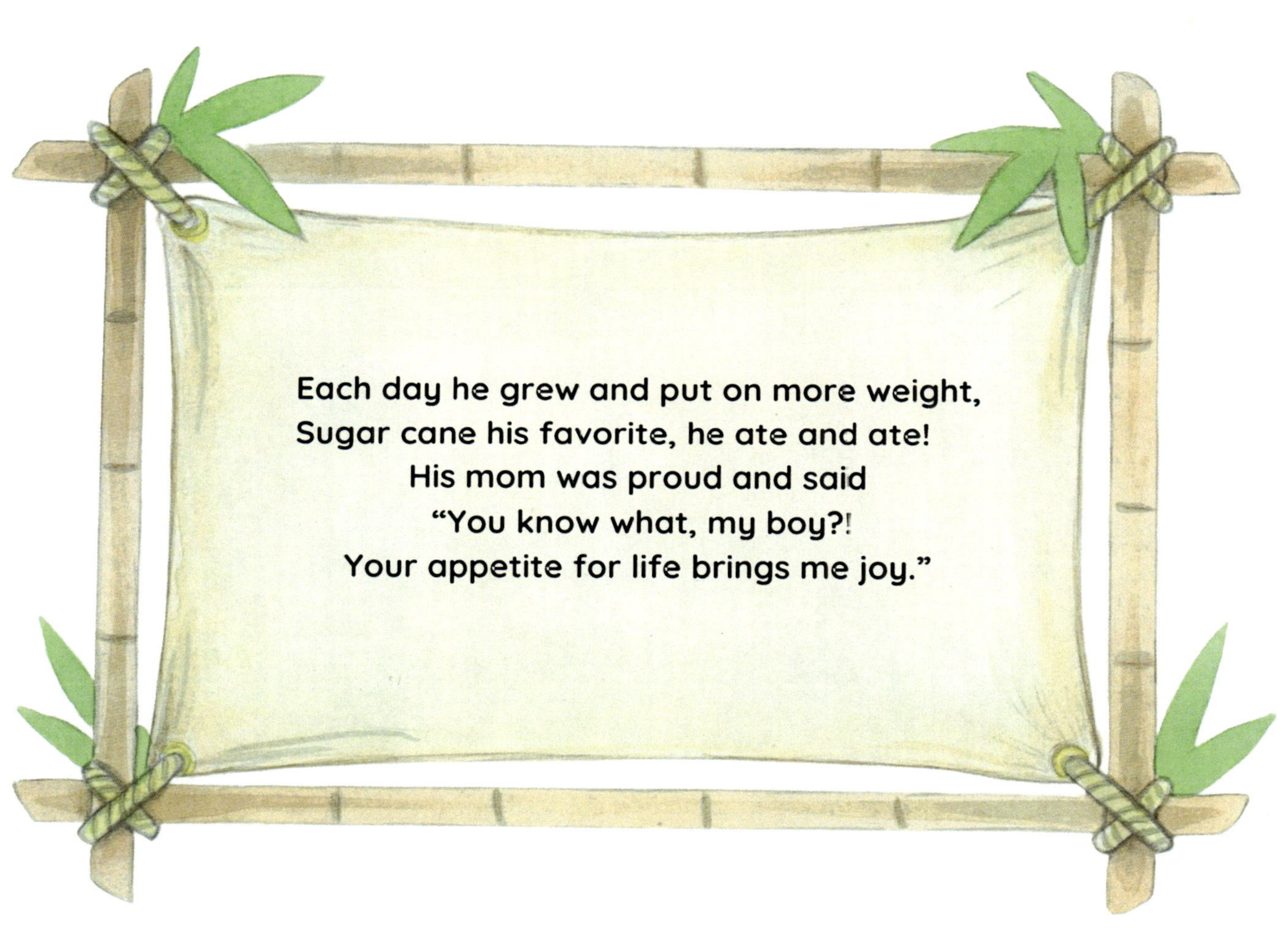
Each day he grew and put on more weight,
Sugar cane his favorite, he ate and ate!
His mom was proud and said
“You know what, my boy?!
Your appetite for life brings me joy.”

"It's time to announce your perfect name!
I will call you my little Chow Mane!"

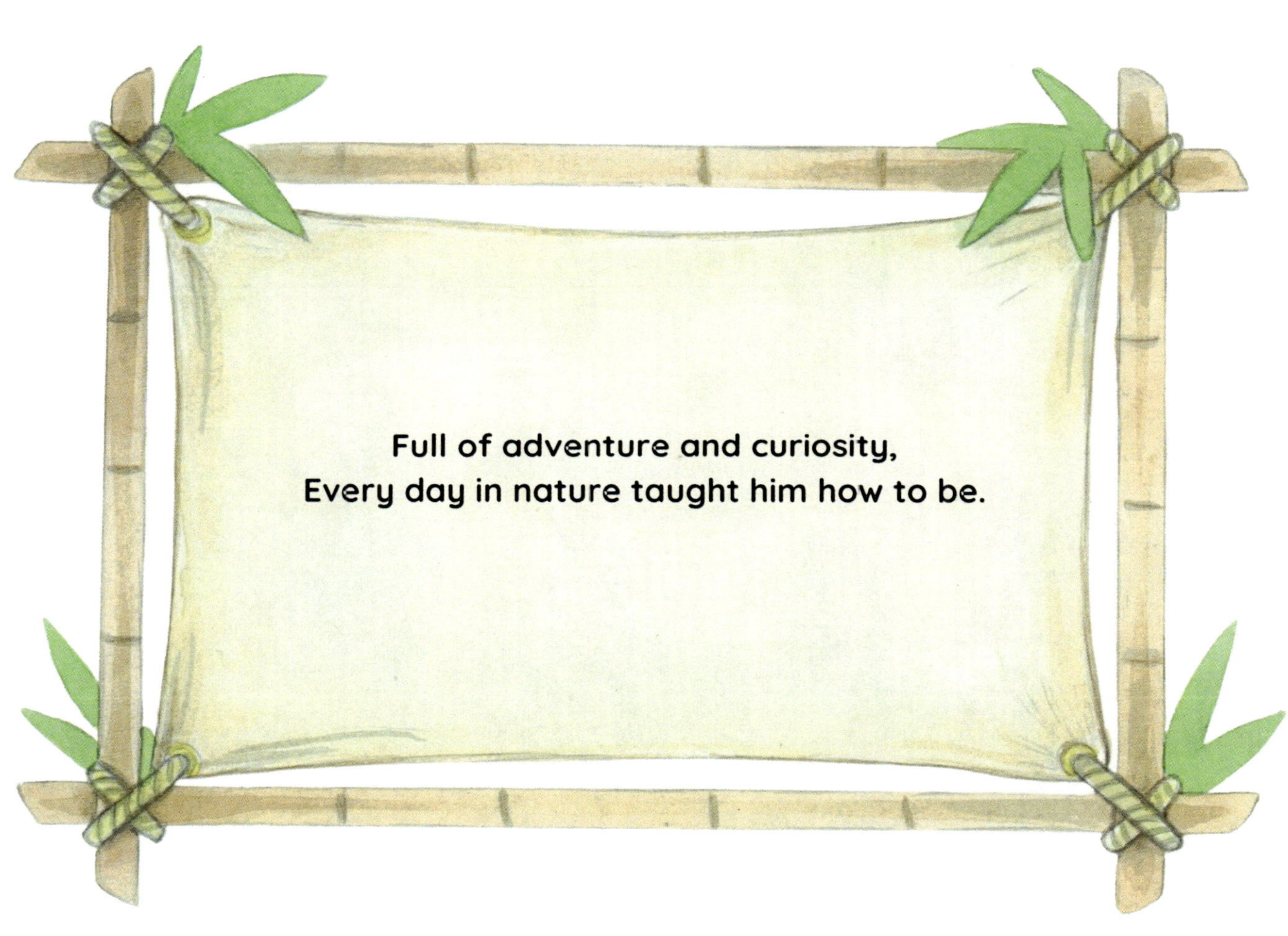

Full of adventure and curiosity,
Every day in nature taught him how to be.

One day without telling his mom,
Chow saw something new and took off on a run.
He darted between a stand of thick trees,
Chasing after some large bumble bees.

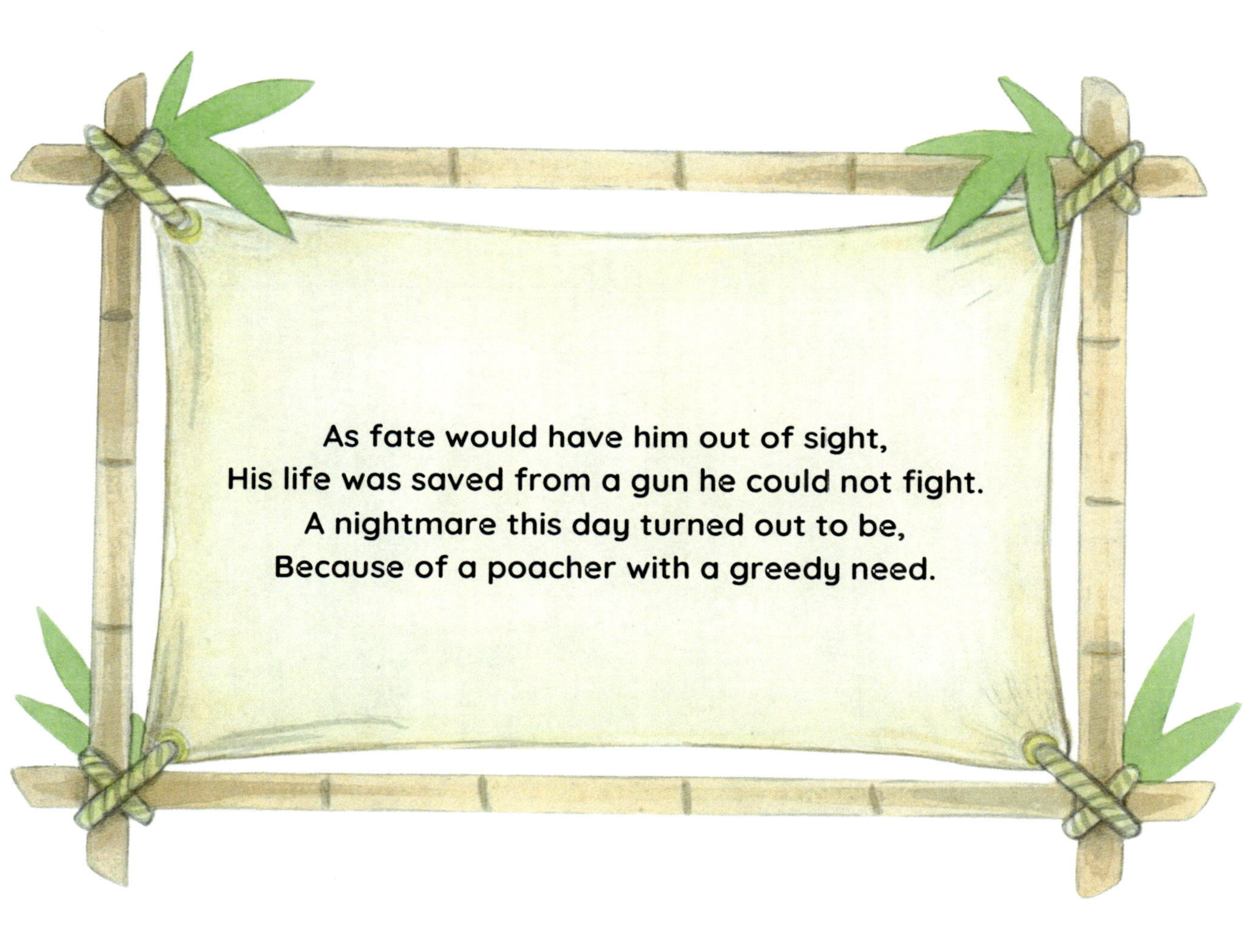

As fate would have him out of sight,
His life was saved from a gun he could not fight.
A nightmare this day turned out to be,
Because of a poacher with a greedy need.

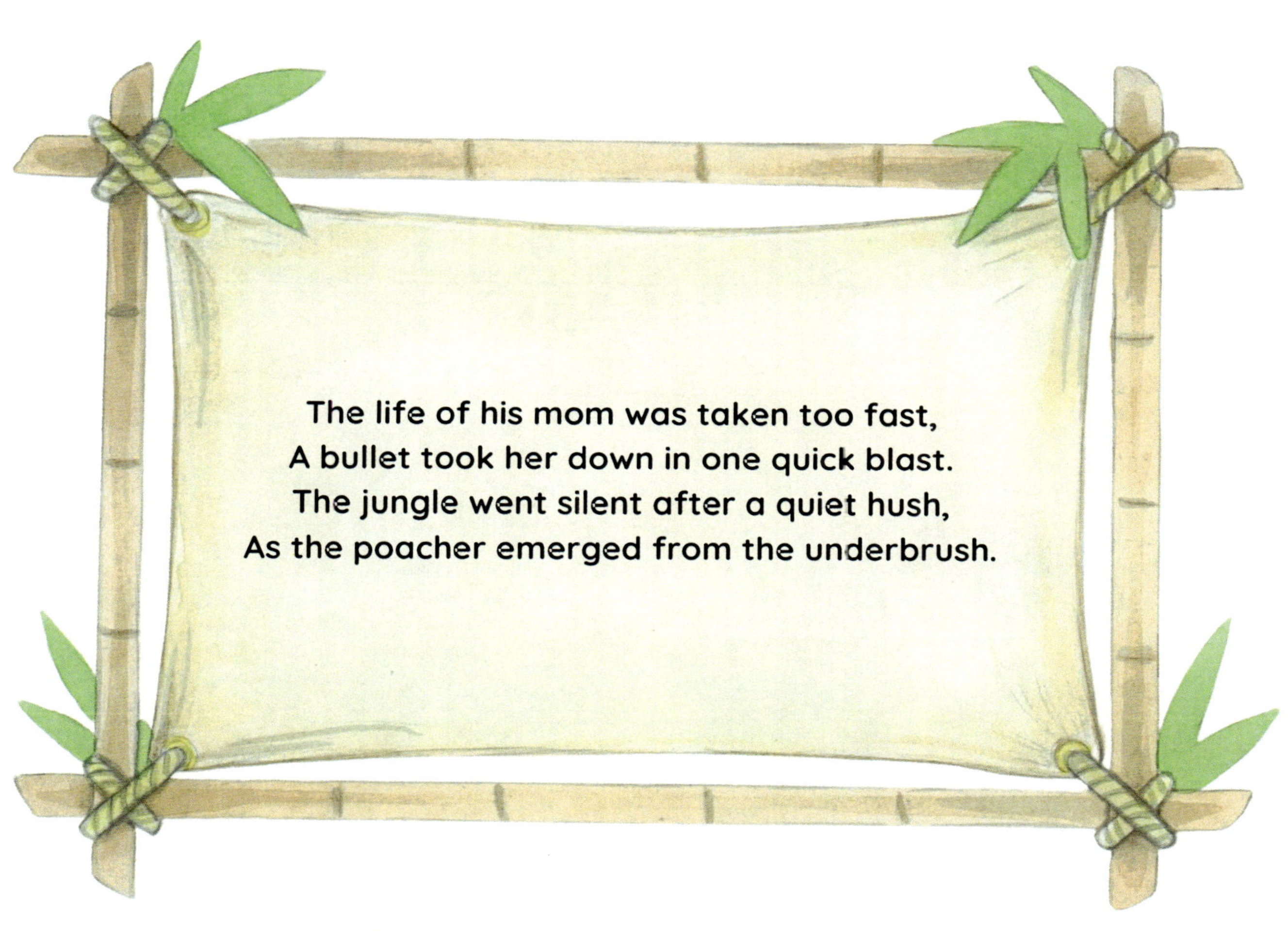
The life of his mom was taken too fast,
A bullet took her down in one quick blast.
The jungle went silent after a quiet hush,
As the poacher emerged from the underbrush.

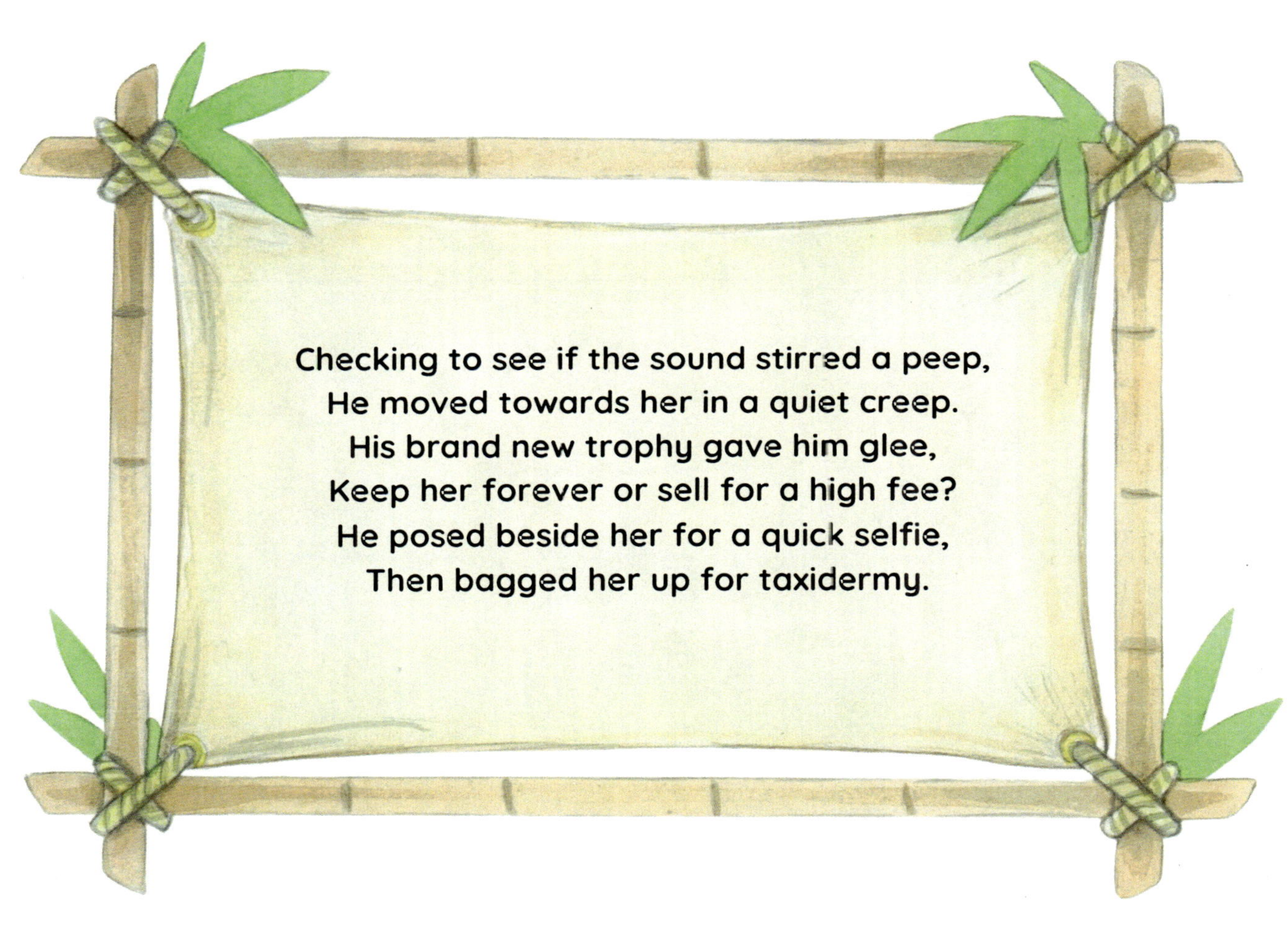
Checking to see if the sound stirred a peep,
He moved towards her in a quiet creep.
His brand new trophy gave him glee,
Keep her forever or sell for a high fee?
He posed beside her for a quick selfie,
Then bagged her up for taxidermy.

The poacher felt smug he didn't get caught,
He was on his way to the black market spot.
But Karma knew, just up ahead,
Payback would return what he dread.

Chow Mane was alone, with no family or friends,
Without rescue, his life could soon meet its end.

SECURITY CAM 3

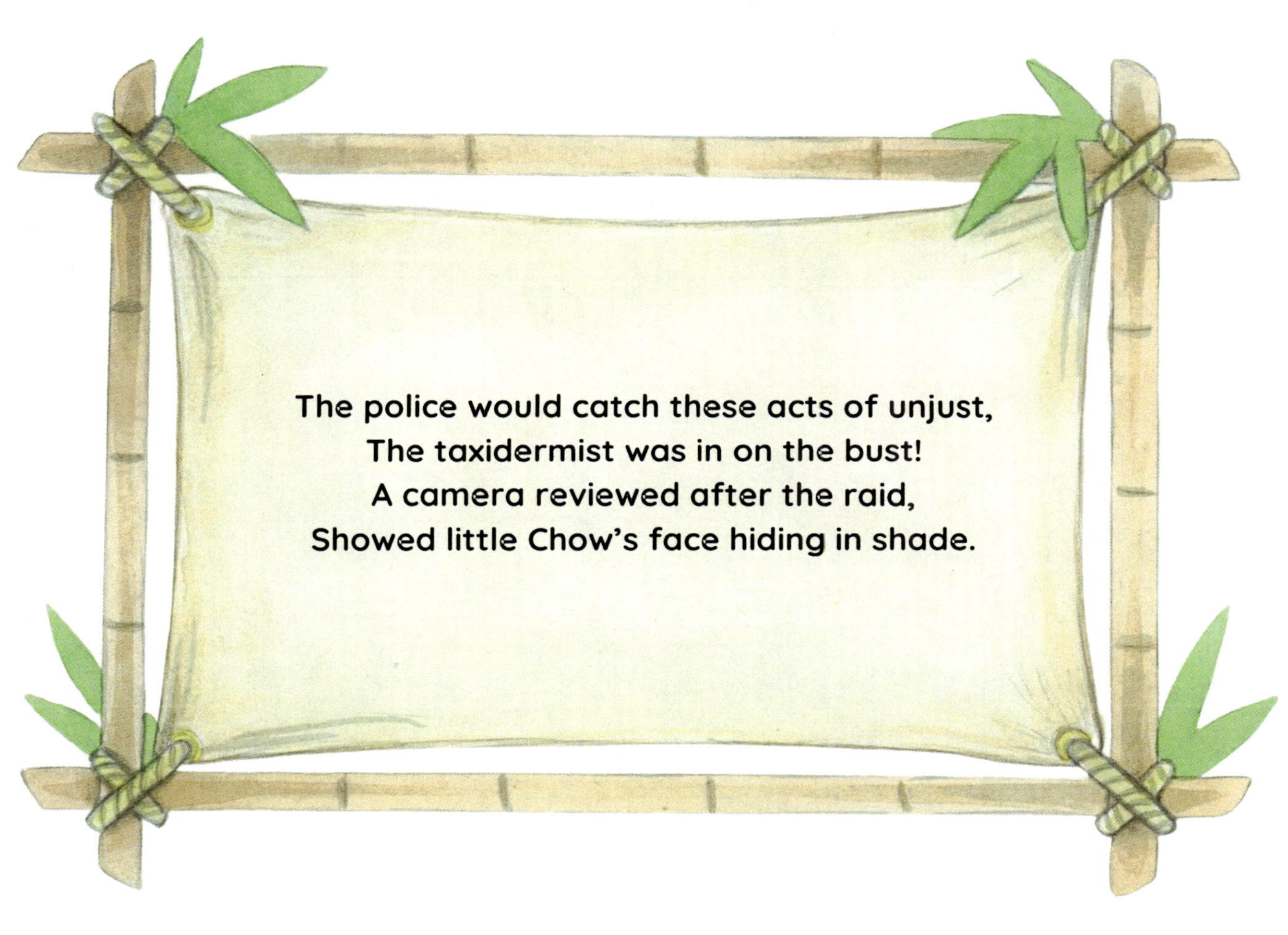

The police would catch these acts of unjust,
The taxidermist was in on the bust!
A camera reviewed after the raid,
Showed little Chow's face hiding in shade.

A rescue team was sent out fast,
Chow Mane was getting help at last.

They took him to a place where animals rehabilitate,
So Chow could rest, recover, and recuperate.

The next day, the sanctuary was happy to see,
And the staff rejoiced with cheer and relief.

Chow Mane was cuddling with two
Animals that is hard to believe.
A local Tiger and even a
Golden Snub Nosed Chimpanzee.
Love is not bound by species or breed,
A chimp, tiger and panda shared a common need.

PANDA SAVED!
POACHER CAUGHT AND ARRESTED!!!
UNLIKELY ANIMAL FRIENDS!
PANDA BROUGHT TO ANIMAL RESCUE AND MAKES NEW BEST FRIENDS!!

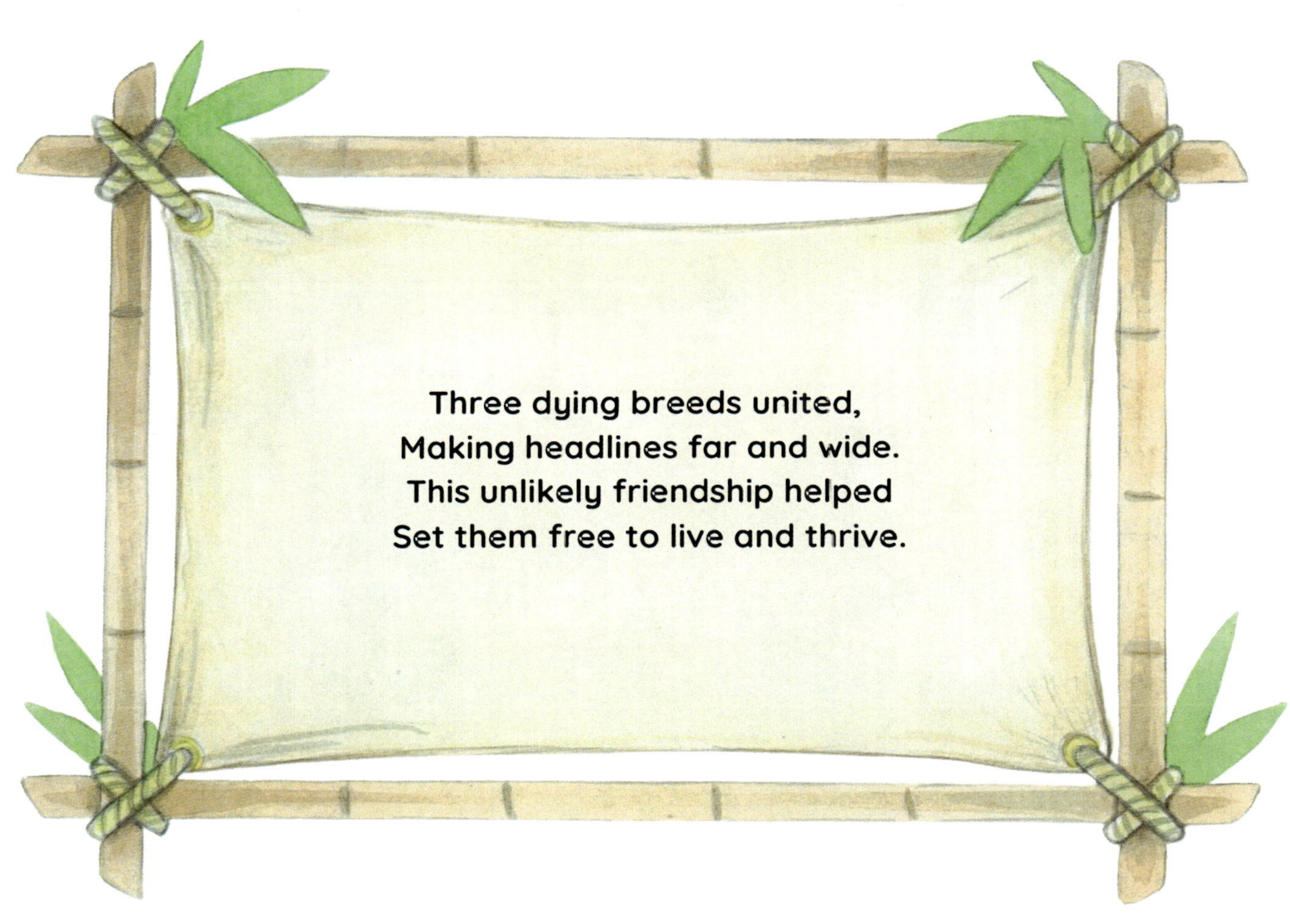
Three dying breeds united,
Making headlines far and wide.
This unlikely friendship helped
Set them free to live and thrive.

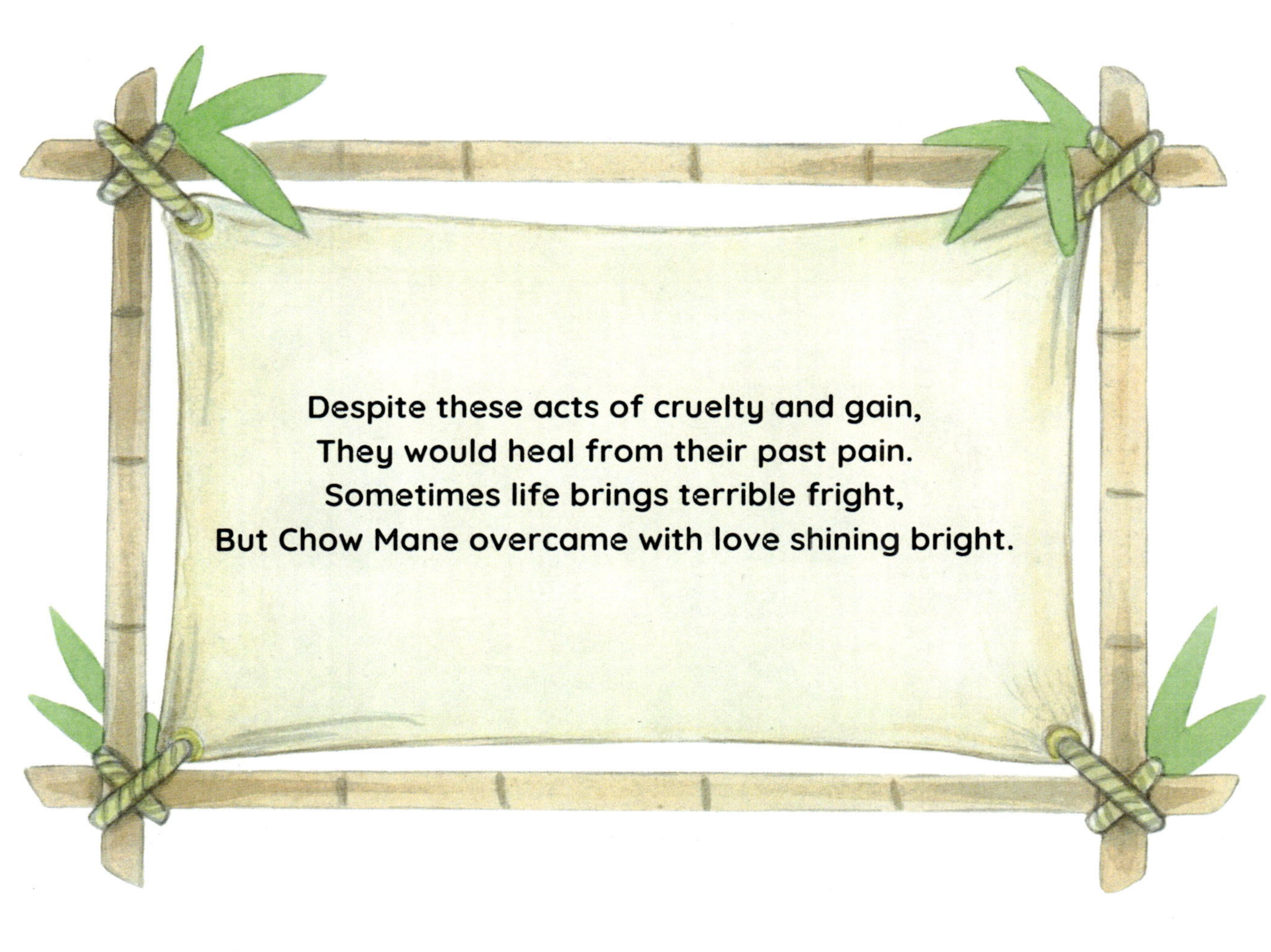

Despite these acts of cruelty and gain,
They would heal from their past pain.
Sometimes life brings terrible fright,
But Chow Mane overcame with love shining bright.

When you feel alone and sad,
Questioning your thoughts "Am I going mad?"

Chow Mane is here to comfort you,
Every dark tunnel has
light when you're through.

Manufactured by Amazon.ca
Acheson, AB

14654405R00029